ISSUE # 7

MONSTER EMOTIONS

MONSTERS HAVE FEELINGS TOO, JUST LIKE YOU

DANNY PETTRY II

DannyPettry.Com, LLC
An Independent Publisher
Beckley, West Virginia

Monster Emotions
Monsters have feelings too, just like you

Published by:
DannyPettry.Com , LLC, Beckley, West Virginia 25801. USA.
DannyPettry.Com provides educational resources and materials for independent learners.

Online: http://www.DannyPettry.com

Book cover designed by *KillerCovers*.

Children's Book.

Printed in the United States of America.

ISBN-13: 978-1511515153

ISBN-10: 1511515155

Cover design by *KillerCovers*.

MONSters

Issues # 7, 8, and 9 were made possible by the generous support from many different people. People who assisted by pledging support via kickstarter or assisting with the video and other promotions were asked to list their name or the name of a loved one in this book. Here they are:

Eliot Parker
Nonie Petrie
Karen Parks
Andrew Horn
Gage and Zoe
Angela Farley
Kristen Wilson
Shawna Green
Wendy Sullivan
Sharon Nichols
Dusten K Fuller
Derric Capteina
Rebekah Walker
Colton Thompson
Renee Oler-Davis
Ryleigh Grace Fink
Ashley Liu Kirkman
Michelle Sutherland
Brody Aaron Dunlap
Stephanie Anderson
Alyssa & Ryan Lively
Jennifer Lynn Propst
Bill & Valerie Hartling
Joker and Cecilia Young
Braydan & Brenna Graham
Amanda Ashleigh Brenwalt
Cooper M. Jarrell. Mason C. Jarrell
Jose Garcia Zoey Augustina Garcia
DaKara Kies - Master Energy Healer
Clayton Thomas Meade & Emily Ann Meade
Victoria and Vaughan Davidson: *KillerCovers*
The Wermers: Paul, Sadie, Shayde, Carver & Ryker
Some supporters asked to remain anonymous.

Picture Credits

Cover design by *KillerCovers*.

Licensed permission to use photos from:
Dollar Photo Club

Picture Name:	Picture created by:	Featured on:
Various Monsters	© BluedarkArt	p. 5
Afraid Monster	© Matthew Cole	p. 6
Angry Monster	© sarah5	p. 7
Anxious Monster	© Matthew Cole	p. 8
Bored Monster	© Matthew Cole	p. 9
Confident Monster	© RA Studio	p. 10
Disappointed Monster	© Peter Hermes Furian	p. 11
Disgusted Monster	© Albert Ziganshin	p. 12
Laughing Vampire	© tawesit	p. 13
Embarrassed Mummy	© VectorShots	p. 13
Excited Monster	© ludimir	p. 14
Frustrated Monster	© sarah5	p. 15
Happy Monster	© musri	p. 16
Hopeful Monster	© ludimir	p. 17
Ignored Monster	© duh84	p. 18
Green Jealous Monster	© Albert Ziganshin	p. 19
Monster with Fish	© RA Studio	p. 19
Lonely Monster	© Matthew Cole	p. 20
Loved Monster	© tigatelu	p. 21
Relaxed Monster	© julien tromeur	p. 22
Sad Monster	© Matthew Cole	p. 23
Shy Monster	© flaya	p. 24
Stress Monster	© Albert Ziganshin	p. 25
Download logo	© djvstock	p. 27

Licensed permission to use one photo from:
CanStockPhoto

Faces	© siamimages	p. 26

MONSTER EMOTIONS

Monsters have feelings too, just like you.

AFraid

Feeling fear and worry

This monster is feeling afraid because she heard a
loud, scary sound.

What was happening when you felt afraid?

Make a face to show how you look
when you're feeling afraid.

Angry

Feeling mad with a person, act, or idea

This monster is feeling angry because someone
called him a name he didn't like.

What was happening when you felt angry?

Make a face to show how you look
when you're feeling angry.

ANXiOUS

Feeling worry, uneasy, or nervous about an upcoming
event or what might happen

This monster is feeling anxious because she is
going to a new school.

What was happening when you felt anxious?

Make a face to show how you look
when you're feeling anxious.

Bored

Feeling like you have nothing to do
or lacking interest in an activity

This monster is feeling bored because there are no
toys in the waiting office.

What was happening when you felt bored?

Make a face to show how you look
when you're feeling bored.

CONFident

Feeing able to do something

This monster is feeling confident that she will win the race in gym class.

What was happening when you felt confident?

Make a face to show how you look when you're feeling confident.

Disappointed

Feeling sad when someone or something did not fulfill your hopes and wishes

This monster is feeling disappointed because the park was closed today.

What was happening when you felt disappointed?

Make a face to show how you look when you're feeling disappointed.

DiSguSted

Feeling sick or extreme dislike

This monster is feeling disgusted because
someone burped at lunchtime.

What was happening when you felt disgusted?

Make a face to show how you look
when you're feeling disgusted.

Embarrassed

Feeling worried about what others might think

This monster is feeling embarrassed because his mummy-wrappings are coming loose and a vampire is laughing at him.

What was happening when you felt embarrassed?

Make a face to show how you look when you're feeling embarrassed.

EXcited

Feeling happy and aroused

This monster is feeling excited because her best friend is coming over to play!

What was happening when you felt excited?

Make a face to show how you look when you're feeling excited.

Frustrated

Feeling stressed when you are not able to
change a situation or solve a problem

This monster is feeling frustrated because he
doesn't understand his homework.

What was happening when you felt frustrated?

Make a face to show how you look
when you're feeling frustrated.

Happy

Feeling pleasure

This monster is feeling happy because she knows
she has a lot of good things in life.

What was happening when you felt happy?

Make a face to show how you look
when you're feeling happy.

HOPEFUL

Feeling good about a future event

This monster is feeling hopeful because she might get a new bicycle for her birthday.

What was happening when you felt hopeful?

Make a face to show how you look when you're feeling hopeful.

Ignored

Feeling like others are not paying attention to you

This monster is feeling ignored because nobody
was listening to him talk.

What was happening when you felt ignored?

Make a face to show how you look
when you're feeling ignored.

JeaLOUS

Feeling upset when someone has something that you would like to have or they get to do something you wanted to do

This monster is feeling jealous because her friend caught a big fish and she didn't.

What was happening when you felt jealous?

Make a face to show how you look when you're feeling jealous.

Lonely

Feeling alone
and that other people do not care about you

This monster is feeling lonely because nobody
played with him at recess.

What was happening when you felt lonely?

Make a face to show how you look
when you're feeling lonely.

Loved

Feeling good because somebody cares about you

This monster is feeling loved because her parents
spend time with her and tell her they love her.

What was happening when you felt loved?

Make a face to show how you look
when you're feeling loved.

ReLaxed

Feeling at ease, calm, and without worries

This monster is feeing relaxed because she is
taking a little nap.

What was happening when you felt relaxed?

Make a face to show how you look
when you're feeling relaxed.

Sad

Feeling sorrow and unhappy about something

This monster is feeling sad
because his kitten ran away.

What was happening when you felt sad?

Make a face to show how you look
when you're feeling sad.

Shy

Feeling nervous or uncomfortable around people

This monster is feeling shy
because it is her first day of school.

What was happening when you felt shy?

Make a face to show how you look
when you're feeling shy.

Stressed

Feeling tense, tired, uneasy, and overwhelmed

This monster is feeling stressed because he has a
lot of homework and chores to do before bedtime.

What was happening when you felt stressed?

Make a face to show how you look
when you're feeling stressed.

What feeling is each of these faces showing?

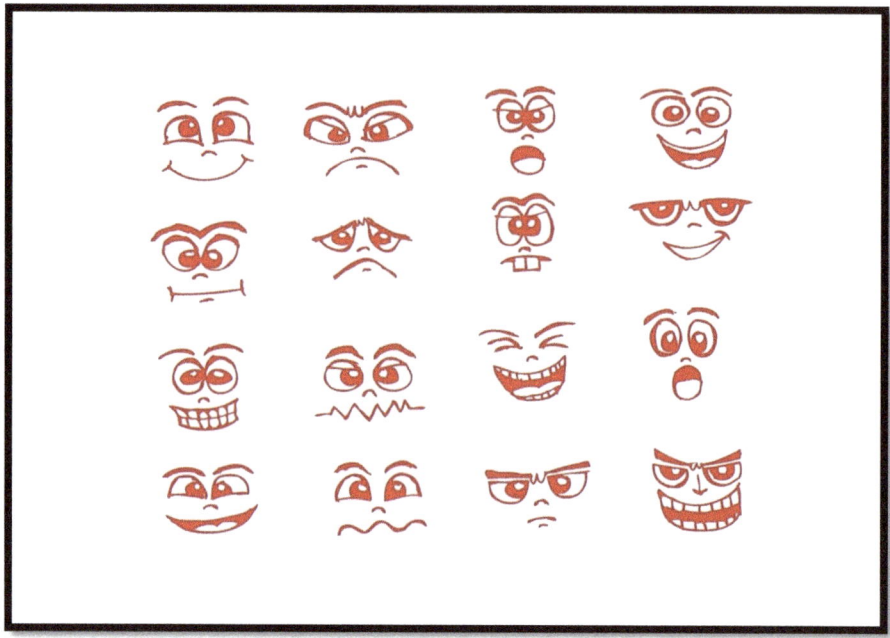

- **What feeling are you having today? Pick a face above if you want to.**

- **Who is a safe person who you can talk to about your feelings?**

- **What are some activities that you can do to cheer yourself up when you're feeling down?**

EXPLOrING EMOTIONS

Activity Book

FREE DOWNLOAD

Download and print an Exploring Emotions Activity Book

This e-book includes 20 activity worksheets that will help children to learn about emotions. Each activity sheet includes one instructor's sheet with discussion questions. This e-book is great for group settings (like classrooms) or for individual use.

Visit this link to download your ebook:
http://www.dannypettry.com/freestuff.html

Danny Pettry II

Danny Pettry is a creative bookmaker.

He loves coffee and conversation.
He also loves reading dystopian novels.

His favorite food is cookies.
His nephew calls him "Uncle Cookie."

He lives in West Virginia.

Email the author: Danny@DannyPettry.Com